SoaringME COMPANION WORKBOOK

The Ultimate Guide to Successful Job Interviewing

M. L. Miller

Published by SoaringME Publishing

ISBN-13: 978-1-956874-08-2

Table of Contents

Introduction

This workbook is designed to be a companion to the book
The Ultimate Guide to Successful Job Interviewing.
Follow the exercises as instructed in preparation for your
upcoming interviews. If you need further explanation of
an exercise, please refer to the companion book.

Begin your preparation a week or two in advance of your
interviews so that you can be thorough. After completing
these exercises it is best to practice your interview
answers to make sure that you are including the
main points that you need to be successful.

Re-constructing the Ideal Profile

List the top ten attributes in bullet point format that you find in Job Advertisements:

Job Ad 1

1 _____

2 _____

3 _____

4 _____

5 _____

6 _____

7 _____

8 _____

9 _____

10 _____

Job Ad 2

1 _____

2 _____

3 _____

4 _____

5 _____

6 _____

7 _____

8 _____

9 _____

10 _____

Job Ad 3

1 _____

2 _____

3 _____

4 _____

5 _____

6 _____

7 _____

8 _____

9 _____

10 _____

Job Ad 4

1 _____

2 _____

3 _____

4 _____

5 _____

6 _____

7 _____

8 _____

9 _____

10 _____

Job Ad 5

1 _____

2 _____

3 _____

4 _____

5 _____

6 _____

7 _____

8 _____

9 _____

10 _____

Job Ad 6

1 _____

2 _____

3 _____

4 _____

5 _____

6 _____

7 _____

8 _____

9 _____

10 _____

Job Ad 7

1 _____

2 _____

3 _____

4 _____

5 _____

6 _____

7 _____

8 _____

9 _____

10 _____

Job Ad 8

1 _____

2 _____

3 _____

4 _____

5 _____

6 _____

7 _____

8 _____

9 _____

10 _____

Job Ad 9

1 _____

2 _____

3 _____

4 _____

5 _____

6 _____

7 _____

8 _____

9 _____

10 _____

Job Ad 10

1 _____

2 _____

3 _____

4 _____

5 _____

6 _____

7 _____

8 _____

9 _____

10 _____

Job Ad 11

1 _____

2 _____

3 _____

4 _____

5 _____

6 _____

7 _____

8 _____

9 _____

10 _____

Job Ad 12

1 _____

2 _____

3 _____

4 _____

5 _____

6 _____

7 _____

8 _____

9 _____

10 _____

Job Ad 13

1 _____

2 _____

3 _____

4 _____

5 _____

6 _____

7 _____

8 _____

9 _____

10 _____

Job Ad 14

1 _____

2 _____

3 _____

4 _____

5 _____

6 _____

7 _____

8 _____

9 _____

10 _____

Job Ad 15

1 _____

2 _____

3 _____

4 _____

5 _____

6 _____

7 _____

8 _____

9 _____

10 _____

Job Ad 16

1 _____

2 _____

3 _____

4 _____

5 _____

6 _____

7 _____

8 _____

9 _____

10 _____

Job Ad 17

1 _____

2 _____

3 _____

4 _____

5 _____

6 _____

7 _____

8 _____

9 _____

10 _____

Job Ad 18

1 _____

2 _____

3 _____

4 _____

5 _____

6 _____

7 _____

8 _____

9 _____

10 _____

Job Ad 19

1 _____

2 _____

3 _____

4 _____

5 _____

6 _____

7 _____

8 _____

9 _____

10 _____

Job Ad 20

1 _____

2 _____

3 _____

4 _____

5 _____

6 _____

7 _____

8 _____

9 _____

10 _____

List up to ten attributes in bullet point format that you see in the backgrounds of profiles that you find on LinkedIn:

Prior background on profile 1

1 _____

2 _____

3 _____

4 _____

5 _____

6 _____

7 _____

8 _____

9 _____

10 _____

Prior background on profile 2

1 _____

2 _____

3 _____

4 _____

5 _____

6 _____

7 _____

8 _____

9 _____

10 _____

Prior background on profile 3

1 _____

2 _____

3 _____

4 _____

5 _____

6 _____

7 _____

8 _____

9 _____

10 _____

Prior background on profile 4

1 _____

2 _____

3 _____

4 _____

5 _____

6 _____

7 _____

8 _____

9 _____

10 _____

Prior background on profile 5

1 _____

2 _____

3 _____

4 _____

5 _____

6 _____

7 _____

8 _____

9 _____

10 _____

Prior background on profile 6

1 _____

2 _____

3 _____

4 _____

5 _____

6 _____

7 _____

8 _____

9 _____

10 _____

Prior background on profile 7

1 _____

2 _____

3 _____

4 _____

5 _____

6 _____

7 _____

8 _____

9 _____

10 _____

Prior background on profile 8

1 _____

2 _____

3 _____

4 _____

5 _____

6 _____

7 _____

8 _____

9 _____

10 _____

Prior background on profile 9

1 _____

2 _____

3 _____

4 _____

5 _____

6 _____

7 _____

8 _____

9 _____

10 _____

Prior background on profile 10

1 _____

2 _____

3 _____

4 _____

5 _____

6 _____

7 _____

8 _____

9 _____

10 _____

Prior background on profile 11

1 _____

2 _____

3 _____

4 _____

5 _____

6 _____

7 _____

8 _____

9 _____

10 _____

Prior background on profile 12

1 _____

2 _____

3 _____

4 _____

5 _____

6 _____

7 _____

8 _____

9 _____

10 _____

Prior background on profile 13

1 _____

2 _____

3 _____

4 _____

5 _____

6 _____

7 _____

8 _____

9 _____

10 _____

Prior background on profile 14

1 _____

2 _____

3 _____

4 _____

5 _____

6 _____

7 _____

8 _____

9 _____

10 _____

Prior background on profile 15

1 _____

2 _____

3 _____

4 _____

5 _____

6 _____

7 _____

8 _____

9 _____

10 _____

Prior background on profile 16

1 _____

2 _____

3 _____

4 _____

5 _____

6 _____

7 _____

8 _____

9 _____

10 _____

Prior background on profile 17

1 _____

2 _____

3 _____

4 _____

5 _____

6 _____

7 _____

8 _____

9 _____

10 _____

Prior background on profile 18

1 _____

2 _____

3 _____

4 _____

5 _____

6 _____

7 _____

8 _____

9 _____

10 _____

Prior background on profile 19

1 _____

2 _____

3 _____

4 _____

5 _____

6 _____

7 _____

8 _____

9 _____

10 _____

Prior background on profile 20

1 _____

2 _____

3 _____

4 _____

5 _____

6 _____

7 _____

8 _____

9 _____

10 _____

Up to fifteen personality traits that your professional network believes fits for this type of job. Put hash marks next to repeated attributes:

1 _____

2 _____

3 _____

4 _____

5 _____

6 _____

7 _____

8 _____

9 _____

10 _____

11 _____

12 _____

13 _____

14 _____

15 _____

Ideal Profile

Compile the top ten skill attributes and top five personality traits that are repeated on your lists. This is the ideal profile.

1 _____

2 _____

3 _____

4 _____

5 _____

6 _____

7 _____

8 _____

9 _____

10 _____

1 _____

2 _____

3 _____

4 _____

5 _____

"So tell me about yourself."
Develop a list of the traits in the Ideal Profile
that overlaps with your experience, skills, and personality traits.
Put the bullet points in chronological order of when
you had that experience or demonstrated that trait.
Practice to keep your answer between thirty and sixty seconds.

1 _____

2 _____

3 _____

4 _____

5 _____

Time permitting:

1 _____

2 _____

Unique Value Proposition (UVP)

Your UVP should be a brief statement that clearly
explains your skills, experience, and unique strengths
in a way that appeals to potential employers.
Focus on bullet points so you don't sound
like a robot that is repeating a rehearsed answer.

1 _____

2 _____

3 _____

4 _____

5 _____

Time permitting:

1 _____

2 _____

Behavioral Questions

Results

Action

Situation

Behavioral Questions

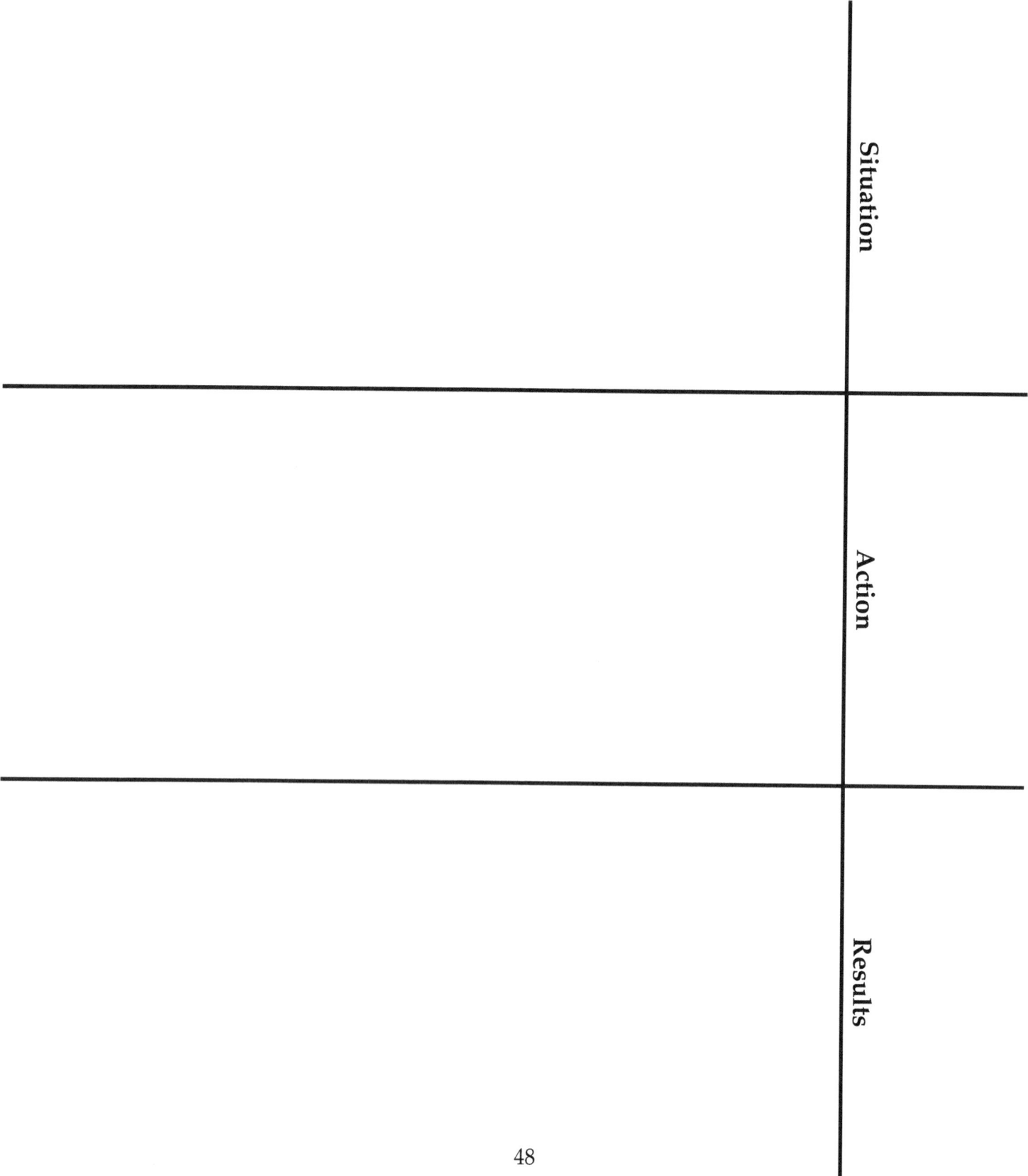

Situation

Action

Results

Behavioral Questions

Results

Action

Situation

Behavioral Questions

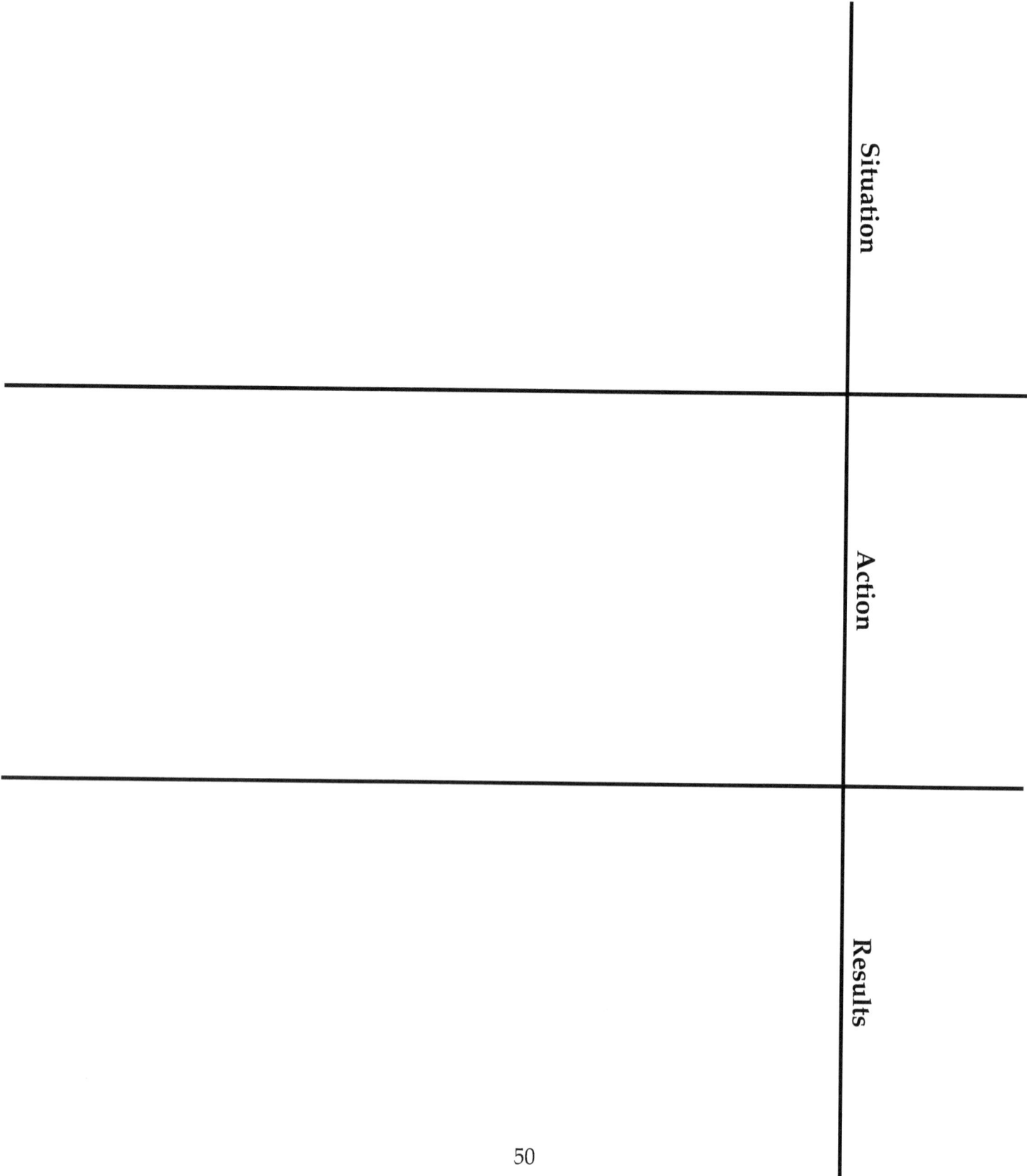

Situation

Action

Results

Behavioral Questions

Results

Action

Situation

Behavioral Questions

Situation

Action

Results

"What is your greatest strength?"
Select three skills, experiences, or traits from the ideal profile
that you have an S.A.R. success story for. Choose one
during the interview to answer this question, and support
your answer with your success story example.

1 _____

S. _____   A. _____   R. _____

2 _____

S. _____   A. _____   R. _____

3 _____

S. _____   A. _____   R. _____

Questions to ask

List your favorite questions from chapter eight that are most relevant to the job or company.

1 _____

2 _____

3 _____

4 _____

5 _____

6 _____

7 _____

8 _____

9 _____

10 _____

Answer/Ask

Based on the ideal profile and your background, list the questions that you are likely to be asked. Then list the relevant question that you can ask after answering them.

1 _____

    Ask: _____

2 _____

    Ask: _____

3 _____

    Ask: _____

4 _____

    Ask: _____

5 _____

    Ask: _____

Answer/Ask

6 _____

    Ask: _____

7 _____

    Ask: _____

8 _____

    Ask: _____

9 _____

    Ask: _____

10 _____

    Ask: _____

Thank you email/note

From chapter seven, construct your thank you email/note.

Items that impressed interviewer:

1 _____

_____

2 _____

_____

Any item that may have concerned interviewer:

1 _____

_____

Express interest in moving to the next step:

1 _____

_____

Thank you email/note

Items that impressed interviewer:

1 _____

_____

2 _____

_____

Any item that may have concerned interviewer:

1 _____

_____

Express interest in moving to the next step:

1 _____

_____

Thank you email/note

Items that impressed interviewer:

1 _____

_____

2 _____

_____

Any item that may have concerned interviewer:

1 _____

_____

Express interest in moving to the next step:

1 _____

_____

Thank you email/note

Items that impressed interviewer:

1 _____

_____

2 _____

_____

Any item that may have concerned interviewer:

1 _____

_____

Express interest in moving to the next step:

1 _____

_____

Thank you email/note

Items that impressed interviewer:

1 _____

_____

2 _____

_____

Any item that may have concerned interviewer:

1 _____

_____

Express interest in moving to the next step:

1 _____

_____

Thank you email/note

Items that impressed interviewer:

1 _____

_____

2 _____

_____

Any item that may have concerned interviewer:

1 _____

_____

Express interest in moving to the next step:

1 _____

_____

Thank you email/note

Items that impressed interviewer:

1 _____

_____

2 _____

_____

Any item that may have concerned interviewer:

1 _____

_____

Express interest in moving to the next step:

1 _____

_____

Thank you email/note

Items that impressed interviewer:

1 _____

_____

2 _____

_____

Any item that may have concerned interviewer:

1 _____

_____

Express interest in moving to the next step:

1 _____

_____

Thank you email/note

Items that impressed interviewer:

1 _____

_____

2 _____

_____

Any item that may have concerned interviewer:

1 _____

_____

Express interest in moving to the next step:

1 _____

_____

Thank you email/note

Items that impressed interviewer:

1 _____

_____

2 _____

_____

Any item that may have concerned interviewer:

1 _____

_____

Express interest in moving to the next step:

1 _____

_____

Ideal Profile adjustments

List any skills, experiences, and traits leaned from interviews

1 _____

2 _____

3 _____

4 _____

5 _____

6 _____

7 _____

8 _____

9 _____

10 _____

Updated Ideal Profile

Adjusted ideal profile based on information learned
in the interview process:

1 _____

2 _____

3 _____

4 _____

5 _____

6 _____

7 _____

8 _____

9 _____

10 _____

1 _____

2 _____

3 _____

4 _____

5 _____

Notes

On the following pages you should keep notes about the feedback that you receive, additional details of the ideal profile, or any other valuable information that you learn throughout the interview process.

Notes

Notes

Notes

Notes

Notes

Notes

Notes

Notes

Notes

Notes

Notes

Notes

Notes

Notes

Notes

www.ingramcontent.com/pod-product-compliance
Lightning Source LLC
Chambersburg PA
CBHW051800200326
41597CB00025B/4626